BOOST YOUR MEMORY

Simple and effective techniques to improve your memory

Written by Gérard Tassignon

Translated by Jessica Foster

Coaching **50MINUTES**.com

BOOST YOUR MEMORY

- **Issue:** how can I stop losing my train of thought during a presentation? How can I remember the name of that person I met during the last networking event? How can I retain that new and interesting piece of information on a particular subject? What techniques can I develop to improve my memory?
- **Uses:** we use our memories on a daily basis to learn and retain a large amount of information. It is therefore indispensable for us to look after them in order to optimise our intellectual faculties.
- **Professional context:** a project or product presentation, professional relationships, professional efficiency, well-being at work, etc.
- **FAQs:**
    - Is it normal to forget things?
    - Why are some memories so easily retained?
    - Does everyone have an equally good memory?
    - Why continue to learn in the age of the internet?
    - How should I go about learning more easily?
    - How can I maintain my memory?
    - I tend to quickly forget what someone has just told me. How can I fix that?

Self-awareness and learning throughout our lives are, in part, characteristics of the human race. All this would certainly not be possible without the unique faculty that is our memory. We have all at some point experienced its limits, however: you are standing in front of a familiar person whose first name eludes you; you have been trying to identify an old school friend for hours; as a student, you have experienced difficulties in the face of the sheer quantity of material to commit to memory during revision and the story sadly repeated itself during your most recent professional training. As you are reading this, you still fear the difficulties that might defy your neurones.

None of the phenomena described above are abnormal. We are not robots! And our memories are fortunately not infallible. Rest assured, in any case, that nothing is unachievable and you can keep learning at any age. Aside from a few medical exceptions, there is no such thing as a fundamentally bad memory. Even better, there are simple ways of developing and improving your memory. Memory is vital to human life. It allows us to learn and adapt throughout our existence, but also to create our own identity. It is therefore essential to take excellent care of it and to take advantage of its full potential.

In 50 minutes, understand how the memory works and learn how to use it at its full capacity thanks to the advice in this short guide. Our exercises, which can be used on a daily basis, will allow you to regain total confidence in your cognitive abilities.

MEMORY: THE BASICS

How it works

The term 'memory' refers to our brains' capacity to analyse and store information in order to reproduce it later. The study of memory, through disciplines such as psychology and neuroscience, has enabled us to outline how it works in three main steps:

- Encoding refers to the learning phase;
- Storage means filing away information;
- Retrieval of information happens when the information is reproduced.

However, this process does not take place through a single system. In fact, everything that is connected to language involves declarative memory (or 'explicit memory'), while the acquisition of motor skills requires procedural memory. In addition, there are three types of distinct memory which work together to ensure that information is passed on and encoded: sensory memory, short-term memory and long-term memory. Memory is also divided between the different parts of the brain:

- the occipital lobe, related to vision;
- the temporal lobe, linked to hearing, smell and balance;
- the parietal lobe, linked to touch;
- and finally the frontal lobe, related to language, movement and to the most complex thoughts and reasoning.

The term 'memory' is therefore multifaceted. Each of its elements is characterised by a different information retention period and a different storage capacity.

A complex, multifaceted mechanism

- **Sensory memory** allows us to interpret the information we receive through our five senses and to retain it for several seconds. It can be subdivided into iconic memory, linked to vision; echoic memory, linked to hearing; olfactory memory, linked to smell; and finally haptic memory, linked to touch. It acts as a filter of the multitude of stimuli to which we are exposed, often subconsciously, and is an obligatory step in information storage.
- **Short-term memory**, also known as working memory, registers active information in our minds temporarily, for the time necessary to complete a task, such as dialling a phone number. The storage capacity of this type of memory is limited to a few moments and, once the task is completed, the data is damaged or lost.
- **Long-term memory** retains the oldest information that is judged to be the most important for an unlimited period of time. It can be divided into implicit and explicit memory. The first is linked to learning memories: riding a bike without thinking about it, for example. The second is the place where memories, strictly speaking, are stored. Explicit memory is divided into semantic memory, for general knowledge, and episodic memory, for our personal memories. We therefore retain a large amount of information subconsciously and only a small amount is recalled consciously. Be careful, however: this memory is

not infallible.

How memory works

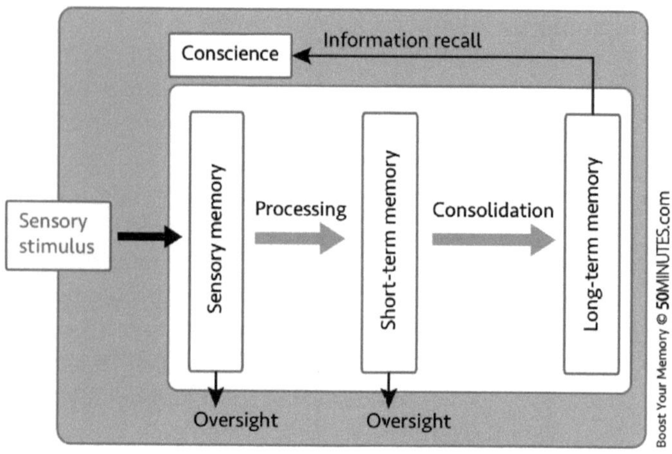

A PERSONAL STRATEGY

Throughout your life – and mainly during your school years – you have undoubtedly adopted, even subconsciously, a particular methodology for retaining information. Setting rhymes to music, mental imagery and mnemonic devices are all effective ways of encouraging learning. But how can we rationalise these things? How can we turn them into a thought-out, organised and reliable process in order to store useful information automatically? Unfortunately, there is not simply one way of doing things that works for everyone; it is each person's job to find their own way by being aware of their capabilities. This is how this booklet can help you.

Here are some simple techniques that can complement your personal strategy and optimise your learning routine:

- Firstly, be aware that you will only retain a piece of information if you think you will use it. It is therefore important to find a purpose for what you wish to learn. You must also discover, if you have not already done so, which method of input works best for you, out of auditory and visual memory, for example.
- Think about increasing the references to yourself and your personal experience. What the psychological researchers Rogers, Kuiper and Kirker call "self-reference" in fact allows us to filter the information that reaches us. It acts as a processing mechanism for information that relates to us. Our perception of data depends on the extent to which it corresponds with the idea that we have of ourselves. Self-reference is very effective, because the "self" defines how the information is dealt with and structured in relation to ourselves.
- Try out mnemonic methods, which are impressively effective. The human brain is designed to more easily retain concrete and figurative ideas than abstract or arbitrary concepts.

SOME MNEMONIC TRICKS

- If you want to remember a list of words, think of a story in which they are all used.
- Use the 'mind palace' technique, which consists of imagining the layout of a familiar place where the different ideas to retain follow on from one

another, in each room or in each different part of the place.
- If you have the mind of an artist, poet or singer, make up your own verse! Nothing is better than rhymes to help you remember something for a lasting period of time.
- Think about putting words in opposition to each other, as this will enable you to put the information into context by creating links.
- Come up with a word made up of the first letters of all the words you want to remember.

Of course, mnemonic techniques are not a miraculous solution for learning, but they are a key strategy for retaining certain one-off elements within a greater whole that has been understood and stored. They are a sort of life belt: you can rely on them when required.

PRIORITISE CONCENTRATION!

Clear your physical and psychological space

Committing anything to your long-term memory is impossible without paying a certain amount of attention. Concentration acts as a filter that amplifies the resonance of information: your brain only retains the information that you think you will use.

However, the simple act of concentrating is often not enough to commit something to your brain's grey matter, even if you isolate yourself from anything that might distract you and distance you from learning methods. To give yourself the best chance possible, consider practising meditation to facilitate your concentration.

As children, we all had to force ourselves to learn poems or texts that we would laboriously recite the next day in front of our classmates. We therefore know the importance of learning 'by heart' in the learning process, as well as its limitations. Both oral and written repetition is necessary for encoding information in our memories. But be careful, don't just parrot off everything! Automatic repetition is only useful for storing information in the short-term memory. It does not allow us to process it in our long-term memory. To do that, we need to establish links between the information that we want to remember and other data that is already stored in the long-term memory. Links established in this way are logical and therefore facilitate the recuperation of information. The depth of the treatment given to the information is therefore essential. Moreover, this point is at the heart of the experiment undertaken in Toronto in 1975 by the researchers Craik and Tulving.

Another important point to highlight is the length of time taken to learn the element in question. Learning something over a long period means it will be better committed to memory than something learned over a short period of time.

Finally, concentration, repetition and duration of learning are supplemented, by many of us, with other techniques such as grouping ideas, mnemonic devices and mental images, as we have previously discussed.

Your grey matter works while you are sleeping

In one of his articles, psychologist Dr Philippe Lambert addresses the close link between sleep and learning. The latter will be affected by poor quality sleep.

First of all, there is tiredness linked to sleep deprivation, which harms concentration and our capacity for attention. But sleep itself also plays a role in the consolidation of cerebral processes. It is therefore essential to sleep in good conditions and in sufficient quantities in order to reach an REM (rapid eye movement) sleep cycle, which is the only one that can truly consolidate our knowledge. Free from external stimuli, the brain can then linger on memories, through dreams. It processes them, organises them, gets rid of them or stores them.

This theory has been proven by many researchers over time. Among the most well-known are the scientist Francis Crick and his colleague, the mathematician Graeme Mitchison, whose hypothesis put forward in 1983 in their co-written article, "The Function of Dream Sleep", explains the role REM sleep, characterised by the frequency and intensity of dreams, plays in the organisation of memories. Dreams, which are mainly active in this cycle, allow us to cut down our interfering or false thoughts from stories, and eliminate them. This premise is also at the centre of research by many other researchers, such as the neuroscientist Jonathan Winson, who illustrated in an article in the *Scientific American* magazine, "The Meaning of Dreams" (1990), that our memories are consolidated in the REM sleep cycle. Even today, Alyson Mary and Philippe Peigneux, postdoc researchers at the *Université Libre de Bruxelles*, have shown in their research that this consolidation process differs between the youngest and oldest members of the population due to the reduction of the amount of REM sleep.

We should not, however, believe that we can learn while we are sleeping. The experiment carried out by Charles Simon and William Emmons in 1955 shows that only drowsiness and the phase separating this from sleep allow us to retain information. On the other hand, no information can be stored during deep sleep, as they show in "The Non-Recall of Material Presented During Sleep".

Exercise as a way of improving your memory

It is no secret to anyone that regular exercise has many health benefits but, more surprisingly, it can also help to improve your cognitive abilities. To optimise these, think about getting out and moving as regularly as possible. Exercise can firstly benefit you by promoting the passage of oxygen to the brain. It also improves the quality of our sleep. But, above all, it allows us to maintain the reflexes of physical activity which frees up cerebral space for intellectual activity. In other words, people who exercise have better psychomotor reflexes and they therefore find it easier to undertake tasks which require control or focus. Studied on rodents, physical exercise stimulates the production of new brain cells in the hippocampus (brain structure located in the temporal lobe that plays a key role in memory and spatial awareness), which enable the brain's development and slow down its ageing process.

Even better, exercising – even only occasionally or for a short amount of time – improves our memory capacity. At least, this is what a study from the Georgia Institute of Technology (USA) states. A 20-minute session of physical exercise between the learning stages can improve the processing of information. The release of the hormone noradrenaline (an organic compound which plays a role in transmitting messages and has different effects depending on the receptors that pick up the substance) during physical exercise could explain these results.

Finally, exercise plays an essential role in the fight against psychological problems such as stress or depression, which are known to seriously harm concentration.

Exercise does not only help us to look after our memories, but also to improve them by enabling learning.

Keep an eye on your diet!

Just like sleep and exercise, diet is a cornerstone of a healthy lifestyle and therefore of full control of our cerebral capacities. Thus, the malnourishment of a child during pregnancy can lead to severe cerebral problems that limit their faculties of attention and concentration. A healthy and varied diet allows the brain to develop perfectly during childhood. Finally, alcohol abuse, the consumption of saturated fats and excesses of caffeine harm sleep quality and therefore impact our concentration. On the other hand, foods rich in vitamins such as fruit, vegetables, antioxidants and polyunsaturated fats such as Omega 3 should be eaten regularly.

As well as the phenomenon of digestion which affects concentration, saturated fats have other, less well-known harmful effects. A recent study from the magazine *Brain, Behaviour and Immunity* highlights the toxic nature of fat for the brain. If our diets are too rich, our microglia – the active immune defence of our central nervous system – will no longer be able to move and will therefore attack our neurones.

There is no one miracle food: only excess is dangerous! The combination of a balanced and varied diet with regular physical exercise allows us to feel good in our bodies and therefore in our minds too. Indirectly, this feeling promotes self-confidence as well as committing new subjects to memory.

TOP TIPS

Here are some simple and effective good resolutions to make, starting today, to turn your memory into your most powerful weapon.

- If your memory is more oral or auditory, consider studying and reading aloud. To train yourself, hide the material and recite it. On the other hand, if you have a more visual memory, try to turn the material you are studying into a diagram or drawing. Close your eyes and see if you can visualise it. Finally, if you need to 'bring your material to life' while you are studying, you have a kinaesthetic memory. Consider creating actions, mimes and expressions to accompany your studies.
- Learn as often as you can. To maintain your memory, use it whenever you are able to: memorise your shopping list, learn your friends' birthdays or telephone numbers off by heart, etc.
- Read! Instead of learning information from watching television, force yourself to read them every day in the press so that you get your neurones working. After reading, see if you can cite the noteworthy facts and the key players in current events. Try to reproduce the outline of each article with the main information. This is the ideal way to exercise your memory on a daily basis.
- Put information in your own words with your own wordplay and idea association. If a piece of information seems too complicated, make sure to adapt it to suit you.
- Exercise your concentration. To be fully attentive and not become distracted, focus on the information.

Certain meditation exercises can improve your ability to concentrate.

- Look after yourself! Your concentration can be affected by an unhealthy lifestyle. Avoid any kind of excess by taking care of your diet and lifestyle. Prevent stress from interfering with your learning by practising meditation.
- Test your memory. Board games such as chess, or crosswords, exercise your brain in a fun way. By practising something new each time, you will test your memory.

FAQS

IS IT NORMAL TO FORGET THINGS?

We all forget things from time to time. Forgetting things is in fact important as it allows our memories to not be saturated by the thousands of stimuli that reach us each day. We therefore sort the data that is useful to us – that which interests us – from that which can be disposed of.

However, failing to remember something does not necessarily mean that it has disappeared; it could have simply not been recalled for a long time and therefore buried beneath a mass of more recent memories. The more a piece of information is researched and contextualised with the aim of being used regularly, the more solidly it will be fixed in our memories.

WHY ARE SOME MEMORIES SO EASILY RETAINED?

"It's like riding a bike, you never forget!"

Some memories seem to be irrepressible, without a conscious effort on our part. Thus, sensorimotor skills, such as riding a bike, swimming or driving, are never forgotten simply because they depend on a different part of our memory than that which is responsible for knowledge, words and images. The latter, known as declarative memory, is the opposite of procedural memory which is linked to motor skills and reflexes. As they are repeated thousands, if not millions of times during our lives, these reflexes are never forgotten, even if our level of ability tends to fall over time.

DOES EVERYONE HAVE AN EQUALLY GOOD MEMORY?

Not everyone is born with the same neural ability. Nonetheless, no scientific study has yet led to the identification of a gene that is particular to geniuses and exceptionally gifted people. It does seem, however, that childhood plays an essential role in the development of memory. The more a child finds their environment stimulating, with many sounds, colours and smells, the more they will develop their memory by giving a meaning to this information. This phenomenon will be accentuated by the reactions that those around them will have in the presence of these stimuli. Finally, memory is improved through use and training. An individual with a lower neural ability can gradually improve their memory through training. It is therefore essential to make an effort when it comes to memory.

WHY CONTINUE TO LEARN IN THE AGE OF THE INTERNET?

Everyone with access to the internet has the power to access a considerable amount of information of any kind. We can therefore legitimately wonder if learning names, events, dates, etc. by heart still makes sense. Would it not be wiser to learn how to search for information properly and to understand it more deeply in order to interpret it? In any case, this idea is at the heart of Don Tapscott's book *Growing*

Up Digital (2008). He believes that by freeing ourselves from learning (in the strict sense of the term) facts such as dates, we can concentrate on understanding the depths and context of the events. Nonetheless, we could easily reply to him that this understanding, much like our capacity to recall and to analyse, needs certain prerequisites as well as a basis of knowledge that only learning can help us to acquire.

HOW SHOULD I GO ABOUT LEARNING MORE EASILY?

The quality of your learning largely depends on the knowledge you have of yourself, your qualities and your weaknesses. Start by organising your work and setting objectives that you judge to be reasonable. In the same way as a strategist, establish a battle plan. Keep the easiest tasks for your quieter moments, and when you feel at your best, focus on the trickier tasks. Focus on the strongest part of your memory, whether it is oral or written, to optimise your studying time. Finally, develop and consolidate your personal techniques.

HOW CAN I MAINTAIN MY MEMORY?

Intellectual and physical activities are essential to maintaining memory. Socialising, leisure time and games generate exchanges which maintain neuronal circuits and therefore improve memory. In this way, dialogue and social exchanges are also beneficial as they require a kind of mental gymnastics. It is therefore important to undertake activities that stimulate memory as often as possible and to vary them as much as possible.

I TEND TO QUICKLY FORGET WHAT SOMEONE HAS JUST TOLD ME. HOW CAN I FIX THAT?

Repetition plays an essential role in information processing. However, this does not have to be repetition in the strict sense of the word. In fact, although repeating something word for word can have its benefits, adapting things by repeating them in your own words or by making personal associations such as with friends, family or experiences, increases the emotional impact of the information received, which also helps it to be processed.

OVER TO YOU

Now that your memory is no longer a secret to you and you know how to make the most of it, take action! Here are some exercises and methods which aim to train you so that you can regain full confidence in your cognitive abilities. Our approach is, of course, not exhaustive and there are plenty of other exercises that you can do on a daily basis to improve your memory. Among the classic methods are crosswords and riddles in newspapers and some televised game shows. Other more common habits such as reading and writing can also help you. Generally, your willingness to learn and your curiosity will be your greatest allies.

FREQUENTLY USING YOUR MEMORY

Rediscover the enjoyment of learning. Memorise information that is as varied as possible, as often as possible. For example, memorise:

- the ten phone numbers you use most frequently
- your ID card number
- your ten best friends' birthdays and numberplates.

Regularly have fun listing presidents, kings and capitals of every region in the world. Train yourself to learn a text that you like, starting with a page containing a few simple lines before increasing the amount until you have learnt the whole text. Jokes or funny stories are naturally an ideal way of learning and will help you to improve your memory while amusing those around you.

REPETITION

When you want to remember a piece of information, consider repeating it to yourself after a short amount of time. Repeat this process a few hours later, the next day, a week later, etc. in order to ensure it has been processed. You will thus see how information is consolidated and becomes established in the long term.

APPROPRIATION

Associate information with figures, places or names that are important to you in order to appropriate it. The more you establish links between what you want or have to retain and your personal life, the more effective the activity of learning will be. Prioritise associations with your passions and your daily routine. For example, if the new door code at work is 3107, associate it with Halloween (31) and the number of days in a week (07). For vocabulary, consider learning by association with synonyms. For more complex information, put it into your own words instead of trying to learn it by heart. You can help yourself to memorise it by explaining it to a friend, or to yourself.

CATEGORISATION

Faced with large amounts of information of all kinds, try to find a running theme in order to organise it into categories and sub-categories that seem logical to you. Proceed methodically to create a classification that makes sense to you. For example, if you are studying 20th-century history, group the events that are linked to politics and the events that you think are more cultural. Thus the year 1969 stands out just as much for the beginning of America's abandonment of the Vietnam War, notably with the Battle of Hamburger Hill, as it does for the Woodstock Festival. If some information is more abstract, focus on first letters, syllables and sounds in order to discern similarities. Consider repeating these different categories aloud so that you remember them well.

USE YOUR IMAGINATION

If you are worried about forgetting to do something, imagine yourself doing it. In the same way as a director, give as much context as you can to the scene with the help of smaller details. Don't be afraid to use your imagination with these anecdotes so that they make an impression on you. If the events of 18 June 1815 (Battle of Waterloo) seem complicated to learn, imagine yourself in the place of Napoleon (or the Duke of Wellington!) in the greatest possible detail.

FURTHER READING

BIBLIOGRAPHY

- Bléandonu, G. (1995) *L'analyse des rêves et le regard mental.* Brussels: Mardaga.
- Craik, F. and Tulving, E. (1975) Depth of Processing and the Retention of Words in Episodic Memory. *Journal of Experimental Psychology.* 104 (3), pp. 268-294.
- Duhamel, A. and Danjean, J.-P. (2014) 7 questions sur la mémoire. *La Vie.* [Online]. September 2014. [Accessed 29 February 2016]. Available from: <http://www.lavie.fr/famille/sante/7-questions-sur-la-memoire-16-09-2014-56187_414.php>
- Gregoire, C. (2013) Bonne mémoire : comment se souvenir de tout (ou presque). *Huffington Post.* [Online]. [Accessed 29 February 2016]. Available from: <http://www.huffingtonpost.fr/2013/10/02/bonne-memoire-comment-se-souvenir-de-tout-ou-presque/>
- Lambert, P. (2015) Vieillissement cognitif : le poids de la nuit. *Tempo Digital.* [Online]. 61. [Accessed 29 February 2016]. Available from: <http://contentviewer.adobe.com/s/Tempo%20Digital/2fd3bd6f-5b71-5351-9f34-30ffba4298bb/Tempo_digital_61_FR/61_cover_fr.html>
- Lavie, P. (1998) *Le monde du sommeil.* Paris: Éditions Odile Jacob.
- Leconte, P., Beugnet-Lambert, C. and Lancry, A. (1988) *Chronopsychologie. Rythmes et activités humaines.* Villeneuve d'Ascq: Presses universitaires de Lille.
- Lieury, A. (2014) Huit questions sur la mémoire.

Sciences Humaines. [Online]. November 2014. [Accessed 29 February 2016]. Available from: <http://www.scienceshumaines.com/huit-questions-sur-lame-moire_fr_33378.html>

- Pigani, E. (1998). Cerveau : 10 questions pour vous rafraichir la mémoire. *Psychologies*. [Online]. October 1998. [Accessed 29 February 2016]. Available from: <http://www.psychologies.com/Bien-etre/Prevention/Hygiene-devie/Articles-et-Dossiers/Cerveau-10-questions-pour-vous-rafraichirla-memoire>
- Raine, L., Lee, H., Saliba, B., Chaddock-Heyman, L., Hillman, C. and Kramer,A. (2013) The Influence of Childhood Aerobic Fitness on Learning and Memory. *PLOS ONE*. [Online]. September 2013. [Accessed 29 February 2016]. Available from: <http://journals.plos.org/plosone/article?id=10.1371/journal.pone.0072666>
- Rogers, T., Kuiper, N. and Kirker, W. (1977) Self-reference and the encoding of personal information. *Journal of Personality and Social Psychology*. 35(9). pp. 677-688.
- Schacter, D. (1996) *À la recherche de la mémoire. Le passé, l'esprit, le cerveau.* Brussels: De Boeck University.
- Sève, M. (2013) Six exercices pour améliorer sa mémoire. *L'Express. L'Entreprise*. [Online]. April 2013 (updated January 2016). [Accessed 29 February 2016]. Available from: <http://lentreprise.lexpress.fr/rh-management/efficacite-personnelle/six-exercices-pour-ameliorer-sa-memoire_1518823.html>

ADDITIONAL SOURCES

- Carter, P. (2005) *The Complete Book of Intelligence Tests.*

West Sussex: John Wiley and Sons Ltd.

- McLeod, S. (2013) Stages of Memory: Encoding, Storage and Retrieval. *Simply Psychology*. [Online]. [Accessed 4 November 2016]. Available from: <http://www.simplypsychology.org/memory.html>
- Mastin, L. (2010) Declarative (Explicit) and Procedural (Implicit) Memory. *The Human Memory*. [Online]. [Accessed 4 November 2016]. Available from: <http://www.human-memory.net/types_declarative.html>
- Higby, K. (1996) *Your Memory: How it Works and How to Improve It*. New York: Marlowe and Company.

50MINUTES.com
History
Business
Coaching
Book Review
Health & Wellbeing
IMPROVE YOUR
GENERAL KNOWLEDGE
IN A BLINK OF AN EYE !
www.50minutes.com